Luxury of the Dispossessed

Dan Duggan

Influx Press, London

Published by Influx Press
Office 3A, Mill Co Project, Unit 3, Gaunson House, Markfield Road
London, N15 4QQ
www.influxpress.com

All rights reserved.
©Dan Duggan 2015

Copyright of the text rests with the author.
The right of Dan Duggan to be identified as the author of this work has been asserted by them in accordance with section 77 of the copyright, designs and patent act 1988.

This book is in copyright. Subject to statutory exception and to provisions of relevant collective licensing agreements, no reproduction of any part may take place without the written permission of Influx Press.

First published 2015

Printed and bound in the UK by the Short Run Press Ltd, Exeter

ISBN 978-1-910312032

This book is sold subject to the condition that it shall not, by way of trade or otherwise, be lent, re-sold, hired out, or otherwise circulated without the publisher's prior consent in any form of binding or cover other than that in which it is published and without a similar condition including this condition being imposed on the subsequent purchaser.

This book is dedicated to my brother and best friend Mike Duggan who has been there for me through all the dark times, without question.

To Alex Cadogan.

And to all those who find themselves on psychiatric wards with no apparent way out.

Contents

10	Acute BLUES
12	Chinese Night
13	A Police State
14	Comics
16	Dress Rehearsal
17	Attic Cross Section
18	The Exhibition
20	Old Horses
22	Dressmaking
23	Blue Flies
24	Not in Comparison
25	Ward Songs
26	Two Black Chairs
28	Brash Ice

29	Oil on Canvas
30	Girl Behind Glass
32	Cigarette Songs
34	Ditch Seminal
36	Bacon on Valium
38	Affective Disorders
40	Arcade Upper Level
41	Supper Songs
42	The End of Summer
44	After Arabic
46	Temporary God
48	A Sentence
50	Acute in the Rain
52	Discharge

boxer.

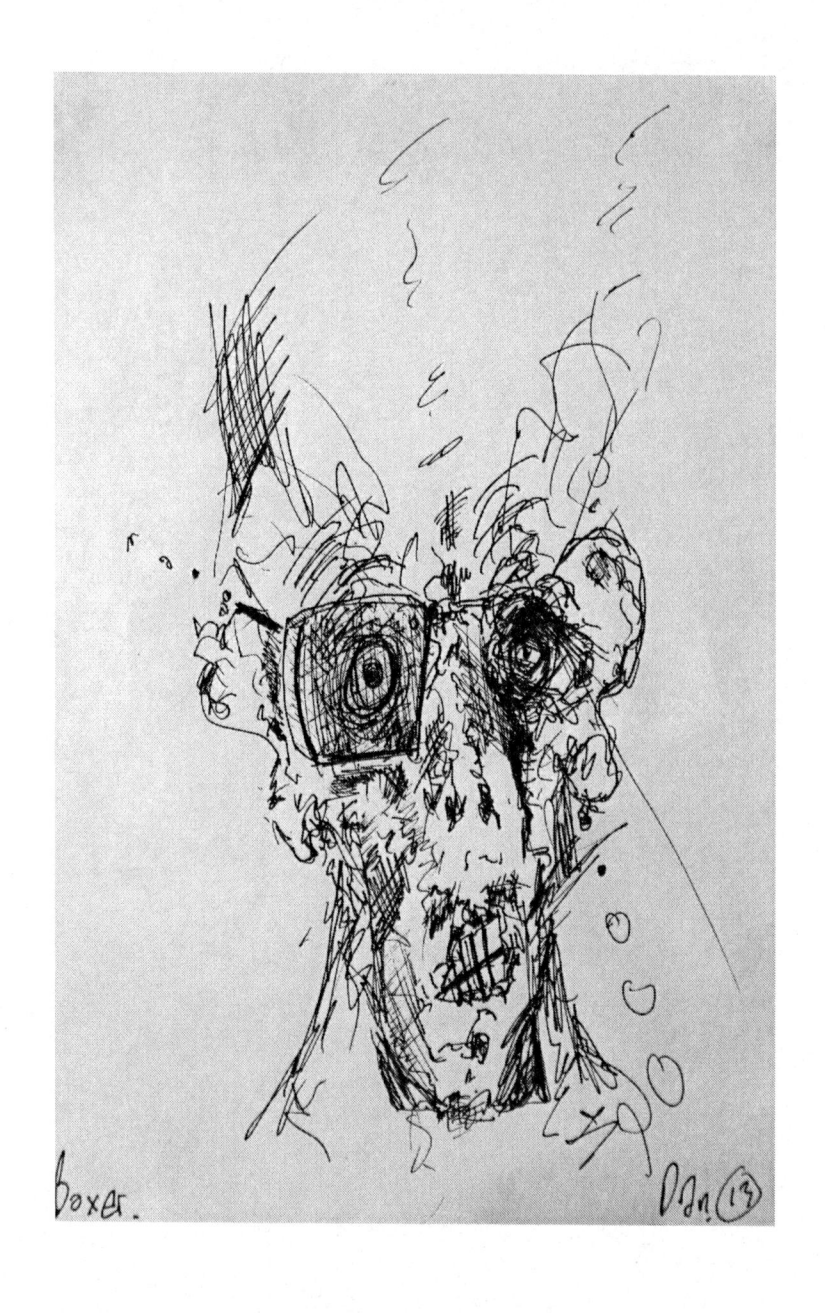

Acute BLUES

(from Green Parks House, Acute Psychiatric)

That first night under section,
they put me in a room overlooking
the hospital garbage, 25 degrees
at night,
the dustcarts arrived at 4am, and
on fourteen mornings subsequent
to this.

Purgatory of a sort. There was blood
in the shower room, so much shit
in every toilet I got used to

antibacterial wipes, seats I scoured
and views over the quadrant.

I had my quarters in Venice I thought,
I had my brother telling me, MOBILES
DON'T RING IN HELL,

then a transistor and sunset, a hot blood
over the sky. I watched my self sleep
face to a fan. My friends gone,
my music lost,

my love inverted.

Chinese Night

(from Green Parks House, Acute Psychiatric)

Lee's been on the Jack and Cokes
all day on an eight hour licence
the doctor gave to him to see his
son and wife. The rest of us, left behind
bet each other that Lee, when he returns,
won't be able to walk down the
blonde corridors without slurring
feet. But he gets back, pulls it off
with the staff, and after dinner and
toast, suggests we get a Chinese, and since
the food is shit, we jump at the chance,
chip in our change, then pretend, once
we're seated over our tinfoil tubs
that the psychiatrists got it wrong once again,
we are Gods.

A Police State

(on failing suicide)

Paramedics, thick set like ivy in
winter, the heavy sane sensible
boots so foreign on your
floors. And the young officer
with his mother doting on his
success. They see the knife in the
chest, attempting to nail love down
but missing by inches and puncturing
a lung. The stretcher won't fit
round the angles of your parents'
stairs. This is not happening all at once.
They have a smell about them these
people, common sense and alcohol
in very equal measures.
They have a grounding beyond your view
right now. They are the ones who will pull
you back into yourself, kicking
and screaming.

Comics

(from the Acute Psychiatric triage ward)

Steve's sketch, did a four year stretch
likes to check that his laces
went the same way as his belt.

(The blues hit me in the day room,
watched some love strip on a loop.)

Then, when you least expect it
toast, hot chocolate and jigsaws.

Steve said God was the number seven or two,
and afterwards nodded to the smoking cage.

We are brave, we are the derelicts.
Our kin buy the shit from the shelves
no one bothers with.

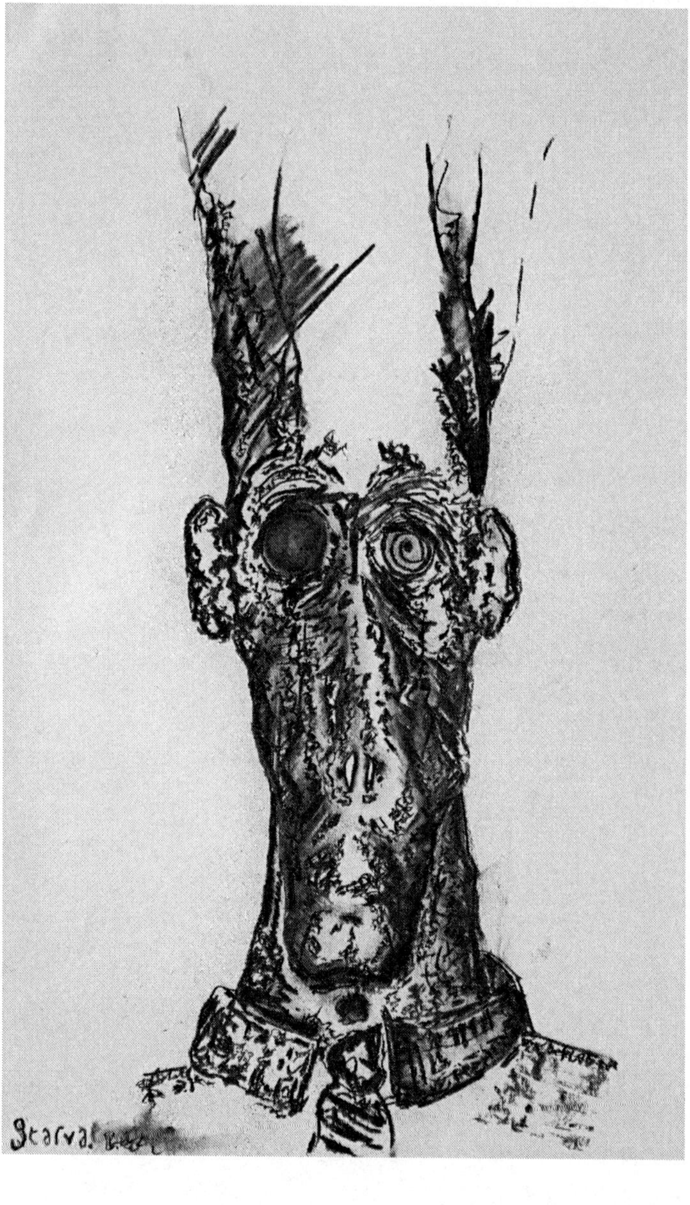
Starva!

Dress Rehearsal

(following a failed suicide attempt)

Chased by security guards around the foyer
of the Royal London Free, in a surgical
gown that didn't fit me, all the flowers
were out, even the dead ones brought
colour to someone's cheeks, I couldn't
recollect, it had been weeks. I had a desire
to go under a bus, where even if the impact
didn't kill you, you'd be drawled on like
a soft flint in summer. They got me back
upstairs, I filched scissors from the apron
of a sister, they let me use a stall alone.

Attic Cross Section

You stole upstairs, stealing each
socked pace like a heartbeat
under cotton.

We saw where you had laid your
sadness, by the roofing gutter
near the heat lamp.

And next morning when we found
you small and damp from
a dream, we had cause

to regret that we'd sent you, without
pause to consider your years,
into the tomorrow we imagined.

The Exhibition

On a bus, two guys from medium secure
and Terry the vocal kind, after many years
inside, inside again but therapeutic, though he
would dispute this and does each week with
the doctors, tells us how many counties
we're passing through. He's robbed some kid
for cash, but gently, never killed or hurt, or
spoiled a couple's date, he hates violence, sort
of a latterday Robin Hood, without the looks.
He dashes off anecdotes about the Solar
System. After two days on painkillers,

I convince myself that by submitting and winning
a place in the exhibition for reprobates, I'm
living the dream. My dad picks
me up on return in a Saab V8. It's too late for
me. I guess suicide attempts in safety
when there were others
to pick up the pieces wasn't enough.
I've got the scars to prove it.
I feel the same about art
as I ever did.

Old Horses

Beneath Cane Hill sanatorium we ate
cold lunches on benches that were meant
for the patients once. And the horses never
galloped in front of us, they had pride
and sanity, straw and water.

These days I wish I'd got into trouble
before the great institutions got mothballed.
It seemed like history would be more appropriate
in a white atrium, than where I lie today beneath

a flat screen broadcasting prescribed tragedy.
I miss those horses. I miss the dream.

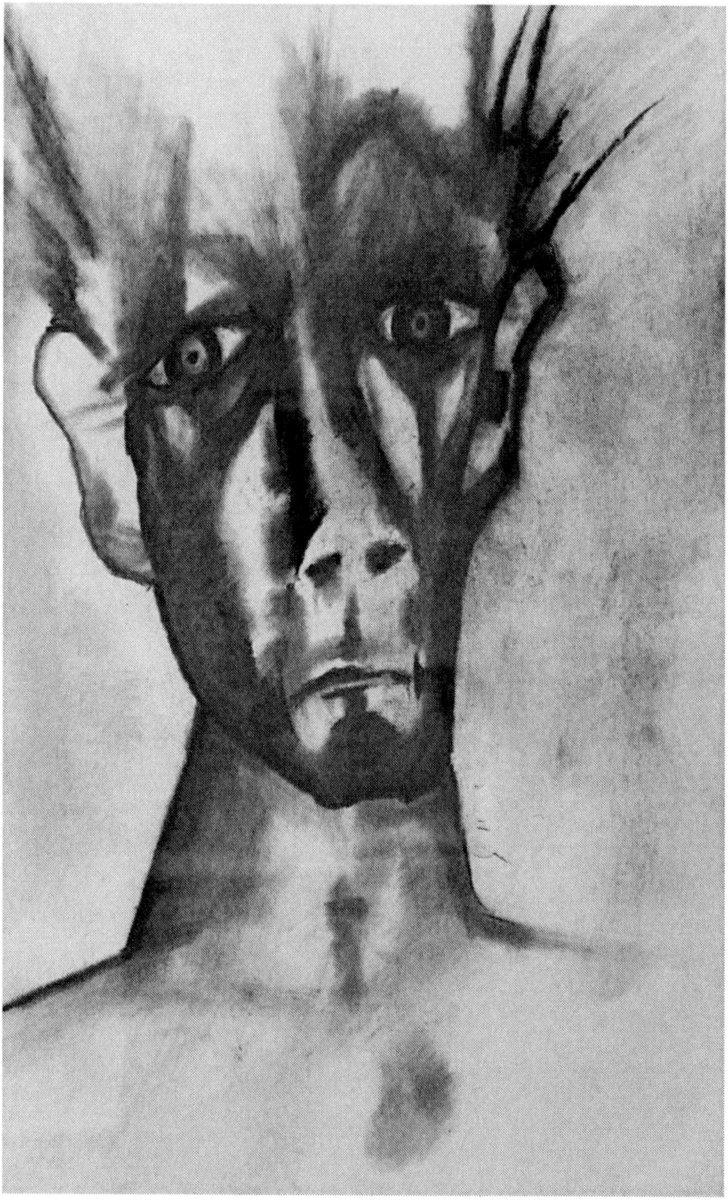

Dressmaking

They laid both wrists face up like
dead fish, and the hour glass over to
the left. A cold bar of sterile

light illuminating the flesh like
sun through a stained glass window.

I watched one stitch, the other follow,
like a corset being tied for a staid evening
of tiresome conversation, a radio, whale

bones, the satin disappearing under caution,
then the neat gasp of satisfaction,
and the finished garment.
It must have been

early morning when they took me to bed . . .

Blue Flies

(Green Parks House, Acute Psychiatric)

They took him to General in high summer.
I slept over the bins, saw him dressed
as fresh as mint each morning.

He couldn't put the lid on the margarine,
even though Arnie encouraged him,
'Steve, now come on Steve . . . '

There were blue flies for him in the dayroom
whilst the domestics vacuumed.

He was a quiet guy, before it dawned on him.

Not in Comparison

(from the eating disorders unit)

They are seated facing each other's
emaciation.
Some have gathered sunlight and lived
on it, others
made do with dust's inattention
to all lights.
And the sight of a room of hunger
is the wonder at the self imposed
upon self.

The Russian soldiers who liberated
Auschwitz had to ration their gifts of food,
to prevent death from over-consumption,
through the sheer madness of starvation.

Ward Songs

Strange how peace returns
its derelicts.
The vacant and extinguished
populate our wards.
But their songs are more
beautiful than the birds,
and each verse, in its infinite
incarceration,
liberates the silence.

Two Black Chairs

A filthy balcony, a sort of colony
for used sun, spent days
and exhaustion.

We watched as it rained,
watched oil gather meridians
and two black chairs

hung with winter's criminal
ice. Those times when life
stops. We came across

each other's wreckage. At times
I wonder if isolation alone
was enough to rob me

of love. We stopped to
watch an opaque glass
force cold water

into a dreadful clarity.

Brash Ice

We coated the windscreen in alcohol
and swore we'd never meet.

I left my cut hair at the feet of a war bronze,
your voice came back to me like

loose change, we pinned our hopes
on disdain remaining. It's a shame the cause

of our love cost the loss. I feel absolutely fine,
summer came, I drank wine beneath the wrists

of a willow, and the wits of spring hung
on the leaves, sort of cried as we must.

Your trust is yours to keep for another.
It's dark now, they are filing the lost.

Oil on Canvas

(from the eating disorders unit)

She's hunched on her windowsill,
a collection of skewed angry bones,
like a pensioner's fist.
She dresses well, looks taught and
everything clings to her in her
distress. They brought the others
down to blackmail her to come
to the dining room.

I am numbed.

Girl Behind Glass

I met this girl called Ellen,
on the local EDU.
In the bloods room,
we made small talk as they
tightened tourniquets.
A wedding ring would have
looked like a bangle on her
wrist. She was obsessed with
care plans, and the letters therein;
what was prescribed to eat
and what she could resist.
I found her fighting a
staff member, over a glass of
orange juice. She claimed it was
written; only water at this time.
I walked up to her, I may have held
her hand, I said Ellen, a care plan
is no good to you when you die, and
I expected some flash of realisation,

like you see in those movies, but
she just looked at me blankly.
I saw her force-fed five times.

About a year after I'd left,
back to see an exhibition,
she was coming down the path from
the ward, with her mum. She looked
like she'd been painted over, with
the thinnest matt pale emulsion.
She passed me, no recognition.
I lit a cigarette, blew smoke into
the ether.

Cigarette Songs

When I saw my second admission
under section the flowers were
either dead or fake. I made a joke

about the way good street drugs
are cut with cynicism. It's afterwards
when we gather to smoke we laugh.

The blackest of humour keeps us free
of need, whatever the doctors
say we require for different reasons.

Someone threw a chair through wired
glass, it looked, after he'd calmed down
like he'd come up with a necklace

on risky threads instead of shoelaces
for the staff. I checked out two days
later with my crumpled Xerox

of what we had and what we lost and
what was left.

Ditch Seminal

That slew of snow we scraped from our boots like
used sheets from an iron-grey typewriter,
that once in a lifetime sense
of self importance, misplaced of course.
But those wonderful days before acute psychiatric,
when I starved and sang in tandem
and the wraps came in comic paper
and the days revolved in a waltz,
have not left the senses now dulled, cold,
any recourse to recollections lost.
It cost, but so does time, stretched,
beaten and hounded.

Deserter.   Don. ⑬

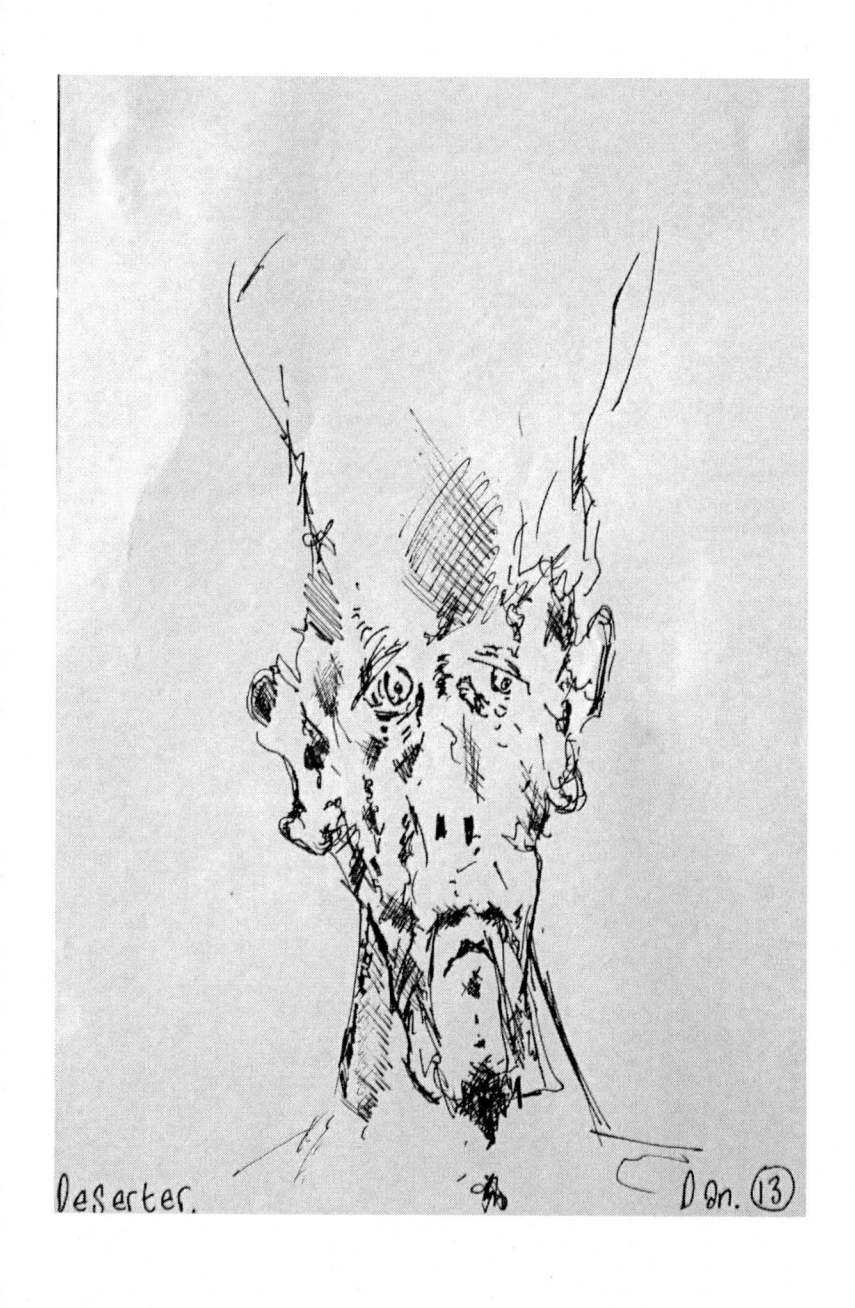

Bacon on Valium

(Acute Psychiatric, midsummer)

Sue worked as an artist, basing
her gift in oils. We were thin.

She said that first day on Acute
I had the looks to make her paint.

I was standing in a hospital towel,
after a shower of sorts, after listening

to the dust trucks haul hospital
garbage into the dawn.

I was seven stone standing.

I think I blushed, said, 'Sue thanks
very much, but the contingency plans

are lost.' She laughed it off and went back to
walking the white night corridors

into the tomorrow she imagined.

Affective Disorders

(Alex. House, The Bethlem Royal Hospital)

May ate panic off the floor whilst
just down the corridor Gordon strode naked
into senility.
Tom called me son each night.
Everyday, except for a brief foray
to the meds queue, he slept
or kept his peace of mind
in solitude.
The gravest error is to mistake
the gratitude for being spared
as sanity.
That is why we are here
not elsewhere.

Stitkch.

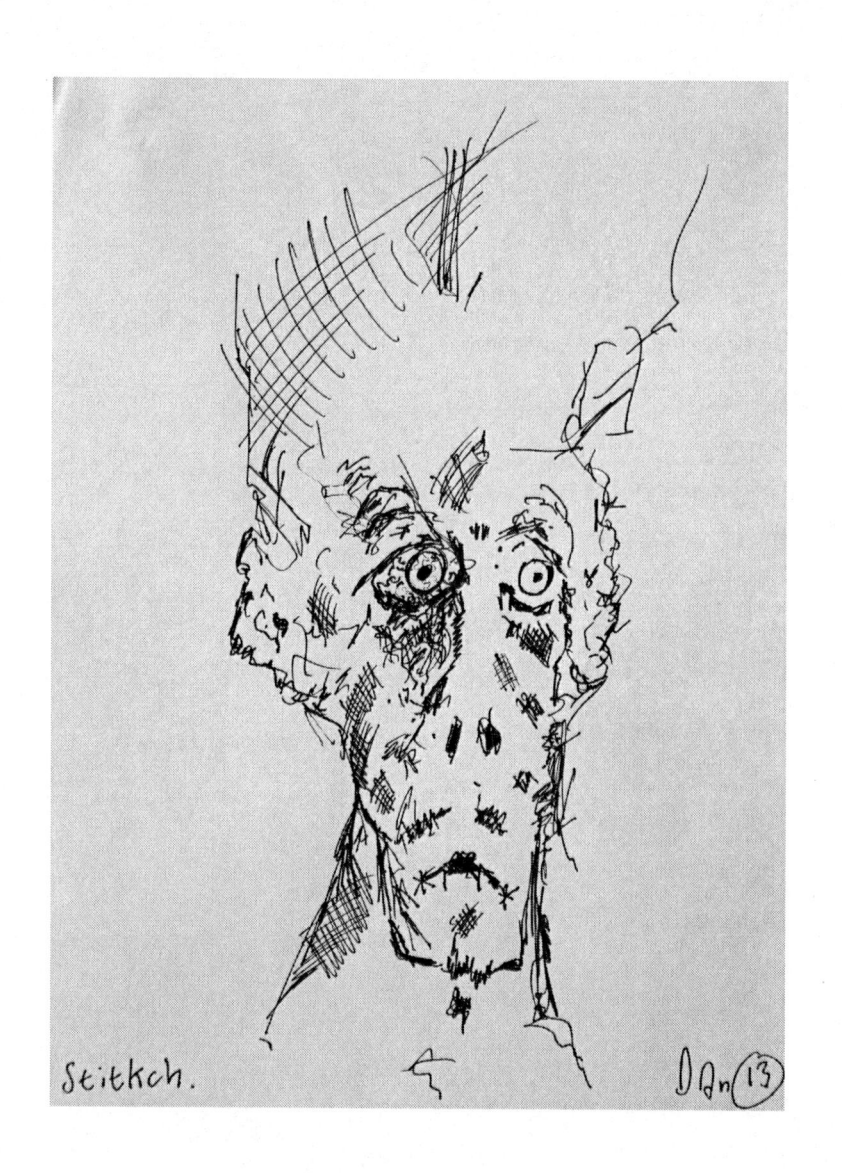

Arcade Upper Level

The neon's got drunk, slurred weakly
over a grey English water.

We watched the prows, distorted
with foam and flotsam
insist upon accuracy.

You can guarantee that in
bad weather they've already collected
crooked silver, the flawed rain.

To relapse quietly is impossible.
Always that terrible rush toward
perfumed parted wrists.

Supper Songs

(from the eating disorders unit)

They have called supper, I can
smell it. My head is shaved,
they found me a corner

where my tiny mouth would
not be noticed. Like a scribbled
full stop trying to devour

the sentence.

The End of Summer

(an arrest for driving drunk and under the influence of psychiatric medication)

They walk me down to the cells,
a green striped room with
a toilet but no visible means
to clean afterwards.

Even water has standards
and perhaps, due to its
clarity, is simply too honest
for such quarters.

Overnight I was watched by
a changing shift, my record or
at any rate what they made
of it, required this.

I have just made a wish list
under the halogens, in light
of the CCTV, to repair to Venice
for the end of summer.

I have an idea death is more
cultured there, might offer a handkerchief,
a view of green lagoons, and, just before
the lock turns, after they've left;
an utter silence you own completely.

After Arabic

Me and Omar swapped evening teabags,
I gave him green, Christ knows what
he gave me. I drank that tea and then
tried to settle down, my heart was beating
so hard, it raised my single white sheet.
I sat up, thought, what in God's name did
he give me? The panic came, not
overt. I went out to see the staff, said,
I feel strange, I can't sleep, my palms,
my heart. So they paged the duty doctor,
1mg of Lorazepam prescribed, I knew
my consultant said he wanted me
not to rely on sedatives, they were addictive
and their efficacy, like a bright winter's
morning, was short lived. So I sat up in that
midsummer hospital room and read certain
Psalms, over and over again, until whatever
Omar gave me cleared my system.
Then I slept. I met him next day, I'd been

told to go home for a week, he'd been told he
was going nowhere. He'd beaten his fists bloody
in frustration. He said, are you going out for a coke?
I said yes, before I head home for a few days,
he said, I don't want a lemonade, get a Red Bull,
Get me two he said. I said no, that's not what you
need right now. He didn't say 'well fuck you then',
just went back to his room, laid down his prayer mat.

Temporary God

That first week on acute, in
high summer, it took three days
for the staff to calm me down,
for the overdose to work through my
system, like sun through a filthy
windshield. I lay still most days.
Once in distress, Grace,
a nurse, prayed over me.
I had my small school New Testament
and Psalms, so after that, after
Arabic with Omar,
I'd sit in the old armchair in
my room and study the Psalms.

I had a mug of green tea and another
day in the furnace was done.
I'm not religious, but some of those
words helped me to morning.
When the dust trucks rolled in at 4am,
it began again.

A Sentence

Two nurses watch me all day.
They watch me at windows, when
I defecate, when I sleep.
It's like pulling a ball and chain,
everything reduced to a clinical
ritual, honest conversation of any
sort, almost impossible.
They found me in the ward bathroom,
I had slit my throat, crimson floor,
some of the staff required counselling.
I had an airlift to the Royal London Free.
I was there three days after they
operated. Then they took me back
to the ward, filthy and desperate,
I was inside four months, no trees,

no fresh air, no sun but what I gathered
through locked windows. I tried
to put a chair through the glass to
breathe, once. So they injected me,
and after that I kept to silence, no point
of reference.

If hope dies last, then
I witnessed it.

Acute in the Rain

(on Section Three of the 1983 Mental Health Act)

The saddest roof, confused with oil,
I stole brushstrokes, the tin foil of
abstract vents and a poor sun.
When you come upon sanity
it seems a trifle, to lose that pivot
on logic the way rain hits water
is to recede gradually like a watercolour.
The saddest tempests I have grown
old in.

It was just six months they said.

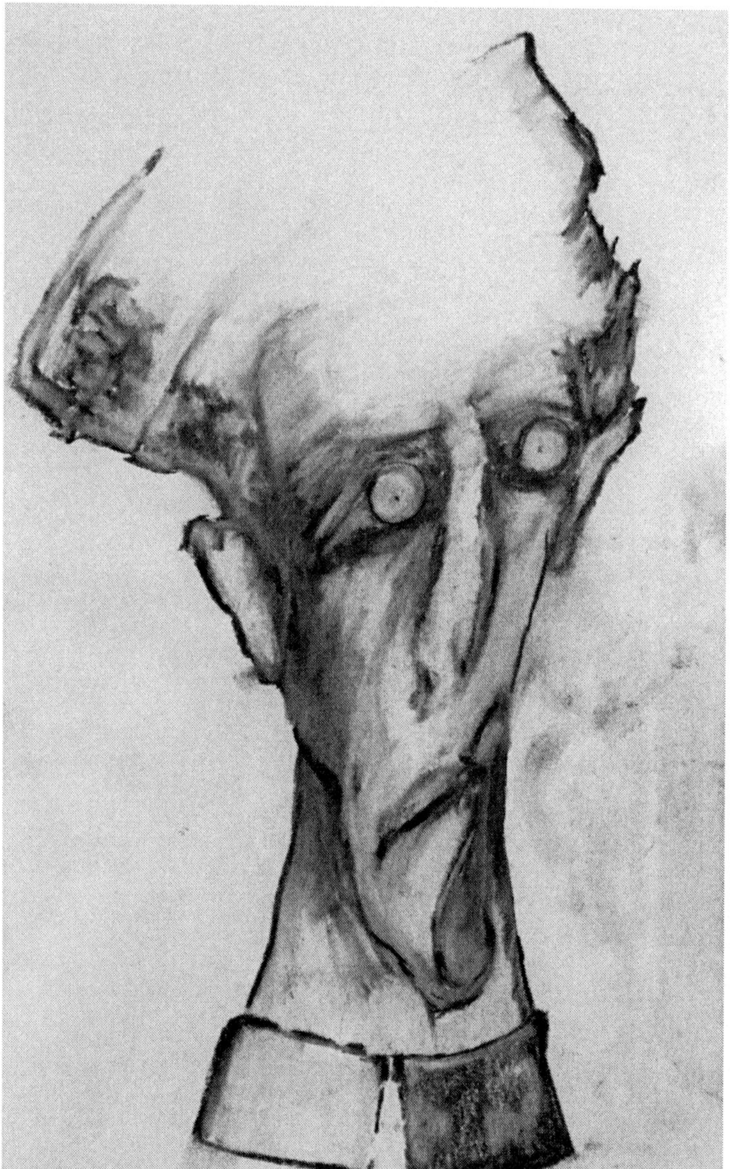

Discharge

Out, the streets look the same,
I approach the Avenue leading
to my parents' home.

I am well, apparently, I am well
according to someone
sipping Chablis in a cool

spot, near where I would have
found peace, or something near
it for days and days done.

Now I find the glass, the smokes,
fond memories of all those
I split cigarettes with,

the lost, the beaten, the disowned.
We called it home, that ward,
out amongst the stars.

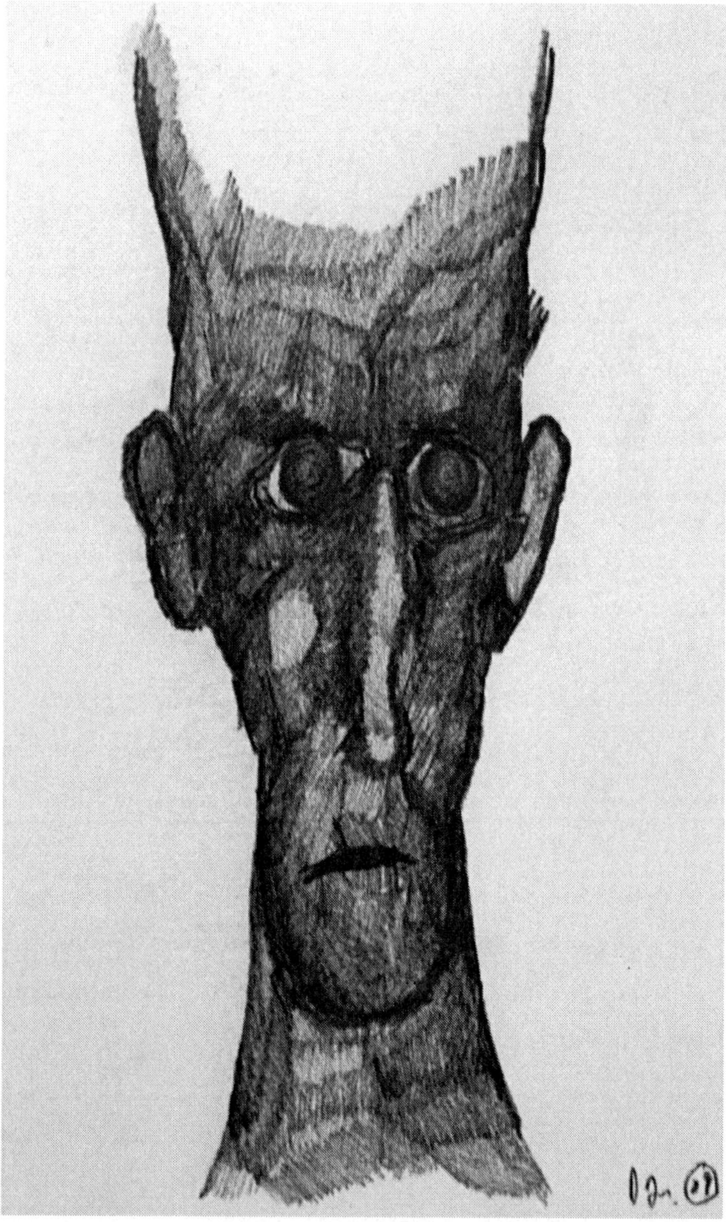

Acknowledgements

I would like to thank Gary Budden and Kit Caless at Influx Press for picking me up, dusting me off and suggesting there could be a book in my poetry and artwork and for all the guidance and support in unknown territory.

I would also like to thank everyone at *Ambit* magazine where many of these poems first appeared, particularly, Liz Berry and Declan Ryan, poetry editors and Briony Bax editor in chief who have always believed in me as a poet and who I also count as good friends.

Also to all my friends, who have been so enthusiastic about the book and given me encouragement and offered kind words.

To Beth Elliot, director of The Bethlem Gallery, who has always supported, encouraged and promoted me as an aspiring artist and who continues to do such amazing work with potential artists with mental health issues.

And last but not least, Martin Bax, the founding editor of *Ambit*.

About the author

Dan Duggan is formerly a patient at The Bethlem Royal Hospital, the oldest pyschiatric hospital in the country. Much of his thirties has been spent on various psychiatric wards, mainly under the provision of the 1983 Mental Health Act. Now in recovery his work has appeared multiple times in *Ambit*, *Poetry and Audience* and *Magma*.

Influx Press is an independent publisher specialising in writing about place.

We publish challenging, controversial and alternative work written in order to dissect and analyse our immediate surroundings, to blur genres and to produce site-specific fiction, poetry and creative non-fiction.

www.influxpress.com